Nuttiest KNOCK-KNOCKS EVER

by MATT RISSINGER
& PHILIP YATES

illustrated by
ETHAN LONG

STERLING

New York / London
www.sterlingpublishing.com/kids

To all the students and staff
at the Crossroads School
— M.R.

To my brother Eddie
— P.Y.

STERLING and the distinctive Sterling logo are registered trademarks of
Sterling Publishing Co., Inc.

Library of Congress Cataloging-in-Publication Data

Rissinger, Matt.
  Nuttiest knock-knocks ever / Matt Rissinger and Philip Yates ; illustrated
by Ethan Long.
    p. cm.
  ISBN 978-1-4027-4256-9
  [1. Knock-knock jokes.] I. Yates, Philip, 1956- II. Long, Ethan. III. Title.
  PN6231.K55R57 2008
  818'.60208--dc22

                                            2008024992

10 9 8 7 6 5 4 3 2 1

Published by Sterling Publishing Co., Inc.
387 Park Avenue South, New York, NY 10016
© 2008 by Matt Rissinger and Philip Yates
Illustrations © 2008 by Ethan Long
Distributed in Canada by Sterling Publishing
c/o Canadian Manda Group, 165 Dufferin Street
Toronto, Ontario, Canada M6K 3H6
Distributed in the United Kingdom by GMC Distribution Services
Castle Place, 166 High Street, Lewes, East Sussex, England BN7 1XU
Distributed in Australia by Capricorn Link (Australia) Pty. Ltd.
P.O. Box 704, Windsor, NSW 2756, Australia

Sterling ISBN 978-1-4027-4256-9

For information about custom editions, special sales, premium and
corporate purchases, please contact Sterling Special Sales
Department at 800-805-5489 or specialsales@sterlingpublishing.com.

CONTENTS

1
NUTTY KNOCK-KNOCKS

KNOCK-KNOCK!
Who's there?
Abandon.
Abandon who?
Abandon the street is
marching this way.

KNOCK-KNOCK!
Who's there?
Aardvark.
Aardvark who?
"Aardvark a hundred miles for one
of your smiles. . . ."

KNOCK-KNOCK!
Who's there?
Abbott.
Abbott who?
Abbott time you answered the door.

KNOCK-KNOCK!
Who's there?
Abner.
Abner who?
Abner noon, pardner.

KNOCK-KNOCK!
Who's there?
Adelia.
Adelia who?
Adelia the cards and we'll play fish!

KNOCK-KNOCK!
Who's there?
Adeline.
Adeline who?
Adeline to a circus and you'll really have a good show.

KNOCK-KNOCK!
Who's there?
Adobe.
Adobe who?
"Adobe, deer, a female deer..."

KNOCK-KNOCK!

Who's there?
Adam.
Adam who?
Adam my way—I'm gonna sneeze.

KNOCK-KNOCK!

Who's there?

Alana.

Alana who?

Alana on my head after I tripped over your skateboard.

KNOCK-KNOCK!
Who's there?
Agatha.
Agatha who?
Agatha feeling you're staring at me.

KNOCK-KNOCK!
Who's there?
Ahab.
Ahab who?
Ahab you seen my sneakers?

KNOCK-KNOCK!
Who's there?
Ahmad.
Ahmad who?
Ahmad you a cake for your birthday.

KNOCK-KNOCK!
Who's there?
Aladdin.
Aladdin who?
Aladdin the street wants to talk to you.

KNOCK-KNOCK!
Who's there?
Alastair.
Alastair who?
Alastair at you if you stare at me.

KNOCK-KNOCK!
Who's there?
Alex.
Alex who?
Alex the questions around here.

KNOCK-KNOCK!
Who's there?
Alfie.
Alfie who?
Alfie you in my dreams!

KNOCK-KNOCK!
Who's there?
Alfred.
Alfred who?
Alfred the needle if you sew the buttons.

KNOCK-KNOCK!
Who's there?
Allen.
Allen who?
Allen a day's work.

KNOCK-KNOCK!
Who's there?
Alpaca.
Alpaca who?
Alpaca trunk. You pack the suitcase.

KNOCK-KNOCK!
Who's there?
Almond.
Almond who?
Almond the wrong side of the law.

KNOCK-KNOCK!
Who's there?
Amahl.
Amahl who?
Amahl shook up!

KNOCK-KNOCK!
Who's there?
Ammon.
Ammon who?
Ammon old hand at fixing things.

KNOCK-KNOCK!
Who's there?
Amnesia.
Amnesia who?
That's funny, I don't remember.

KNOCK-KNOCK!
Who's there?
Amora.
Amora who?
Amora I see, the less I like.

KNOCK-KNOCK!
Who's there?
Anatole.
Anatole who?
Anatole me you'd be coming over today.

KNOCK-KNOCK!
Who's there?
Anka.
Anka who?
Anka the ship.

KNOCK-KNOCK!
Who's there?
Antoine.
Antoine who?
One Antoine are two!

KNOCK-KNOCK!
Who's there?
Appall.
Appall who?
Appall night worrying about this test.

KNOCK-KNOCK!
Who's there?
Archibald.
Archibald who?
Archibald so now he wears a wig.

KNOCK-KNOCK!
Who's there?
Arizona.
Arizona who?
Arizona room for one
of us in this town.

KNOCK-KNOCK!
Who's there?
Armani.
Armani who?
Armani is all spent, so now we're poor.

KNOCK-KNOCK!
Who's there?
Armor.
Armor who?
Armor snacks coming? I'm starving.

KNOCK-KNOCK!
Who's there?
Amory.
Amory who?
Amory Christmas and a Happy New Year!

KNOCK-KNOCK!
Who's there?
Arnie.
Arnie who?
Arnie reasons why this door is always locked?

KNOCK-KNOCK!
Who's there?
Arthur.
Arthur who?
Arthur mometer is broken.

KNOCK-KNOCK!
Who's there?
Asia.
Asia who?
Asia gonna ask me out tonight?

KNOCK-KNOCK!
Who's there?
Athena.
Athena who?
Athena mouse run past your door!

KNOCK-KNOCK!
Who's there?
Atlas.
Atlas who?
Atlas my true love has arrived.

KNOCK-KNOCK!
Who's there?
Augusta.
Augusta who?
Augusta wind blew the leaves off the trees.

KNOCK-KNOCK!
Who's there?
Aurora.
Aurora who?
Aurora's just come from the basement. Go downstairs and see if there's a lion on the loose.

KNOCK-KNOCK!
Who's there?
Author.
Author who?
Author any more candy bars?

KNOCK-KNOCK!
Who's there?
Avery.
Avery who?
Avery time I knock, you ask me the same questions.

2
WHO DARE?

KNOCK-KNOCK!
Who's there?
Barbara.
Barbara who?
"Barbara black sheep, have you any wool?"

KNOCK-KNOCK!
Who's there?
Bacon.
Bacon who?
Bacon a cake for your
birthday.

KNOCK-KNOCK!
Who's there?
Bargain.
Bargain who?
Bargain up the wrong tree.

KNOCK-KNOCK!
Who's there?
Baron.
Baron who?
Baron mind who
you're talking to.

KNOCK-KNOCK!
Who's there?
Bashful.
Bashful who?
Sorry, I can't tell you.
I'm too embarrassed.

KNOCK-KNOCK!
Who's there?
Bassoon.
Bassoon who?
Bassoon things
will be much better.

KNOCK-KNOCK!
Who's there?
Bea.
Bea who?
Bea dear and open the door.

KNOCK-KNOCK!
Who's there?
Beezer.
Beezer who?
Beezer black and yellow,
and they make honey.

KNOCK-KNOCK!
Who's there?
Beta.
Beta who?
Beta be good, 'cause Santa Claus
is coming to town.

KNOCK-KNOCK!

Who's there?

Bettina.

Bettina who?

Bettina minute you'll open this door.

KNOCK-KNOCK!

Who's there?

Ben.

Ben who?

Ben standing here for an hour, open the door.

KNOCK-KNOCK!
Who's there?
Biggish.
Biggish who?
No, thanks, I'll take the smallest shoe.

KNOCK-KNOCK!
Who's there?
Blush.
Blush who?
Thanks; but I didn't sneeze.

KNOCK-KNOCK!
Who's there?
Bobbin.
Bobbin who?
Bobbin the pool and he can't swim.

KNOCK-KNOCK!
Who's there?
Bobsled.
Bobsled who?
Bobsled down the steps
and broke his arm.

KNOCK-KNOCK!
Who's there?
Bolivia.
Bolivia who?
Bolivia me—I know what I'm talking about.

KNOCK-KNOCK!
Who's there?
Booty.
Booty who?
Booty and the Beast is my
favorite movie.

KNOCK-KNOCK!
Who's there?
Brent.
Brent who?
I'm totally Brent out of shape.

KNOCK-KNOCK!
Who's there?
Brewsters.
Brewsters who?
Brewsters go "cock-a-doodle-do!"

KNOCK-KNOCK!
Who's there?
Burglar.
Burglar who?
Wait a minute.
Burglars don't knock.

3
KNOCKETY-KNOCK!

KNOCK-KNOCK!
Who's there?
Caesar.
Caesar who?
Caesar quickly before
she gets away.

> **KNOCK-KNOCK!**
> Who's there?
> Callous.
> Callous who?
> Callous if you need directions.

KNOCK-KNOCK!
Who's there?
Carlotta.
Carlotta who?
Carlotta trouble when it breaks down.

KNOCK-KNOCK!
Who's there?
Candy.
Candy who?
Candy cow jump over
the moon?

KNOCK-KNOCK!
Who's there?
Cassie.
Cassie who?
Cassie the forest for the trees.

KNOCK-KNOCK!
Who's there?
Cauliflower.
Cauliflower who?
Cauliflower, but it won't answer.
Why not?
'Cause flowers can't talk!

KNOCK-KNOCK!
Who's there?
Cecile.
Cecile who?
Cecile this envelope
before you mail it.

KNOCK-KNOCK!
Who's there?
Celeste.
Celeste who?
Celeste time I lend you anything!

KNOCK-KNOCK!
Who's there?
Census.
Census who?
Census Saturday, we don't
have to go to school.

KNOCK-KNOCK!
Who's there?
Cereal.
Cereal who?
Cereal pleasure to meet you.

KNOCK-KNOCK!

Who's there?

Chesterfield.

Chesterfield who?

Chesterfield full of sheep.

KNOCK-KNOCK!
Who's there?
Claudette.
Claudette who?
Claudette a whole container of ice cream.

KNOCK-KNOCK!
Who's there?
Cola.
Cola who?
Cola doctor. I think I'm gonna pass out.

KNOCK-KNOCK!
Who's there?
Column.
Column who?
Column down. Things will be all right.

KNOCK-KNOCK!
Who's there?
Commit.
Commit who?
Commit me and we'll go places.

KNOCK-KNOCK!
Who's there?
Cosmo.
Cosmo who?
Cosmo trouble than it's worth.

KNOCK-KNOCK!
Who's there?
Costas.
Costas who?
Costas a fortune to get here.

KNOCK-KNOCK!
Who's there?
Cowhide.
Cowhide who?
Cowhide if
he sees you
coming.

KNOCK-KNOCK!

Who's there?
Crispin.
Crispin who?
Crispin and
crunchy is how I
like my cereal.

KNOCK-KNOCK!

Who's there?
Crypt.
Crypt who?
Crypt past your window last night,
but I didn't see you.

KNOCK-KNOCK!

Who's there?
Cynthia.
Cynthia who?
Cynthia been away, I've missed you.

4
RAP RAP!

KNOCK-KNOCK!
Who's there?
Dakota.
Dakota who?
Dakota is too long
in the arms.

KNOCK-KNOCK!
  Who's there?
Daisy.
  Daisy who?
Daisy plays, nights he sleeps.

KNOCK-KNOCK!
  Who's there?
Dale.
  Dale who?
Dale be big trouble if you don't open the door.

KNOCK-KNOCK!
  Who's there?
Danielle.
  Danielle who?
Danielle at me. It's not my fault.

KNOCK-KNOCK!
  Who's there?
De Niro.
  De Niro who?
De Niro I am to you, the better I like you.

KNOCK-KNOCK!
Who's there?
Decay.
Decay who?
Decay is after de J and before de L in the alphabet song.

KNOCK-KNOCK!
Who's there?
Deduct.
Deduct who?
Deduct who went "Quack Quack!"

KNOCK-KNOCK!
Who's there?
Deepen.
Deepen who?
Deepen is where you find de pig.

KNOCK-KNOCK!
Who's there?
Defeat.
Defeat who?
Defeat are hurting. Can I come in and sit down?

KNOCK-KNOCK!
Who's there?
Degrade.
Degrade who?
Degrade I got on my spelling test wasn't so good.

KNOCK-KNOCK!
Who's there?
Delta.
Delta who?
Delta great hand of cards.

KNOCK-KNOCK!

Who's there?

Desiree.

Desiree who?

Desiree of sunshine in my life.

KNOCK-KNOCK!

Who's there?

Despair.

Despair who?

Despair of sneakers makes my feet stink.

KNOCK-KNOCK!

Who's there?

Dexter.

Dexter who?

"Dexter halls with boughs of holly."

KNOCK-KNOCK!

Who's there?

Diego.

Diego who?

Diego before de B.

KNOCK-KNOCK!
Who's there?
Disarm.
Disarm who?
Disarm hurts from knocking.

KNOCK-KNOCK!
Who's there?
Disease.
Disease who?
Disease pants fit you?

KNOCK-KNOCK!
Who's there?
Disguise.
Disguise who?
Disguise been following me
since I stepped on his toe.

KNOCK-KNOCK!
Who's there?
Dish.
Dish who?
Dish must be a world record
for knocking.

KNOCK-KNOCK!
Who's there?
Dispatch.
Dispatch who?
Dispatch of pumpkins is huge!

KNOCK-KNOCK!
Who's there?
Distress.
Distress who?
Distress was on sale; do you like it?

KNOCK-KNOCK!
Who's there?
Donald.
Donald who?
"Donald come baby, cradle and all."

KNOCK-KNOCK!

Who's there?

Donalette.

Donalette who?

Donalette the bed bugs bite.

5
KNOCK VERY FUNNY!

KNOCK-KNOCK!
Who's there?
Ear He.
Ear He who?
Ear He feeling. This place is haunted.

KNOCK-KNOCK!
Who's there?
Easily Distractible.
Easily Distractible who?
I'm sorry, were you talking to me?

KNOCK-KNOCK!
Who's there?
Eddie.
Eddie who?
Eddie body home?

KNOCK-KNOCK!
Who's there?
Emile.
Emile who?
Emile fit for a king.

KNOCK-KNOCK!
Who's there?
Eliza.
Eliza who?
Eliza wake at night thinking
about monsters.

KNOCK-KNOCK!
Who's there?
Ernest.
Ernest who?
Ernest is where a birdie lives.

KNOCK-KNOCK!
Who's there?
Elsie.
Elsie who?
Elsie you later!

KNOCK-KNOCK!
Who's there?
Esau.
Esau who?
Esau him come in through the window.

KNOCK-KNOCK!
Who's there?
Europe.
Europe who?
Europe to no good, aren't you?

KNOCK-KNOCK!
Who's there?
Eyesore.
Eyesore who?
Eyesore do like you.

KNOCK-KNOCK!
Who's there?
Fang.
Fang who?
Fang you very much, that's the nicest thing anyone has ever said to me.

KNOCK-KNOCK!
Who's there?
Ferdie.
Ferdie who?
Ferdie last time—open the door!

KNOCK-KNOCK!
　　Who's there?
Ferris.
　　Ferris who?
Ferris fair. So don't cheat.

KNOCK-KNOCK!
　Who's there?
Fido.
　Fido who?
Fido known you were coming
I'd have baked a cake.

46

KNOCK-KNOCK!
  Who's there?
Fitzwilliam.
    Fitzwilliam who?
Fitzwilliam better than it fits me.

  KNOCK-KNOCK!
    Who's there?
  Formosa.
      Formosa who?
  Formosa the summer I was
  on vacation.

KNOCK-KNOCK!
  Who's there?
Fozzie.
    Fozzie who?
Fozzie hundredth time—
my name is Henry.

KNOCK-KNOCK!

Who's there?

Foster.

Foster who?

Foster than a speeding bullet.

KNOCK-KNOCK!

Who's there?

Furry.

Furry who?

"Furry's a jolly good fellow."

6
DOOR STOPPERS!

KNOCK-KNOCK!
Who's there?
Gable.
Gable who?
Gable to leap tall buildings
in a single bound.

KNOCK-KNOCK!
Who's there?
Gas.
Gas who?
Gas again. I can't figure it out either,
so your gas is as good as mine.

KNOCK-KNOCK!
Who's there?
Gauze.
Gauze who?
'Gauze it's important to exercise.

KNOCK-KNOCK!

Who's there?

Gargoyle.

Gargoyle who?

Gargoyle twice a day to prevent gingivitis.

KNOCK-KNOCK!
Who's there?
General Lee.
General Lee who?
General Lee, I don't mind the
school cafeteria food.

KNOCK-KNOCK!
Who's there?
Geometry.
Geometry who?
Geometry in the school play,
but I wish I were a flower.

KNOCK-KNOCK!
Who's there?
Gibbon.
Gibbon who?
Gibbon the circumstances,
I'd rather stay home.

KNOCK-KNOCK!
Who's there?
Goliath.
Goliath who?
Goliath down on the hammock.

KNOCK-KNOCK!
Who's there?
Gopher.
Gopher who?
Gopher a swim in the lake.

KNOCK-KNOCK!
Who's there?
Gretel.
Gretel who?
Gretel long, little doggie.

KNOCK-KNOCK!
Who's there?
Gwenna.
Gwenna who?
Gwenna phone
rings, answer it!

7
KNOCK-ORTUNITIES!

KNOCK-KNOCK!
Who's there?
Hair combs.
Hair combs who?
Hair combs the judge!

> **KNOCK-KNOCK!**
> Who's there?
> Halibut.
> Halibut who?
> Halibut a kiss on the cheek?

KNOCK-KNOCK!
Who's there?
Hank.
Hank who?
You're welcome.

KNOCK-KNOCK!
Who's there?
Harmony.
Harmony who?
Harmony times do I have to tell you
to stop picking your nose?

KNOCK-KNOCK!
Who's there?
Hanover.
Hanover who?
Hanover all your money.

KNOCK-KNOCK!
Who's there?
Harriet.
Harriet who?
Harriet so much ice cream,
he got sick to his stomach.

KNOCK-KNOCK!
Who's there?
Hatch.
Hatch who?
Gesundheit!

KNOCK-KNOCK!
Who's there?
Heifer.
Heifer who?
Heifer dime is better than
half a penny.

KNOCK-KNOCK!
Who's there?
Henrietta.
Henrietta who?
Henrietta snack and ruined her appetite.

KNOCK-KNOCK!
Who's there?
Heywood, Hugh, and Harry.
    Heywood, Hugh, and Harry who?
Heywood Hugh Harry up and
open the door?

KNOCK-KNOCK!
Who's there?
Hideout.
    Hideout who?
Hideout you even thought it
was possible.

KNOCK-KNOCK!
Who's there?
Honeydew.
    Honeydew who?
Honeydew you want to come out tonight?

KNOCK-KNOCK!
Who's there?
Hoyt.
    Hoyt who?
Hoyt myself riding a bicycle.

KNOCK-KNOCK!
Who's there?
Hugo.
Hugo who?
Hugo wherever you want to go!

KNOCK-KNOCK!
Who's there?
Ice cream soda.
Ice cream soda who?
Ice cream soda the
whole world knows
I'm watching a
scary movie.

KNOCK-KNOCK!

Who's there?

Ida.

Ida who?

Ida written sooner, but I lost your address.

KNOCK-KNOCK!

Who's there?

Iguana.

Iguana who?

Iguana hold your hand.

KNOCK-KNOCK!

Who's there?

Imogen.

Imogen who?

Imogen life without ice cream.

KNOCK-KNOCK!
Who's there?
Iowa.
Iowa who?
Iowa lot to my big brother.

KNOCK-KNOCK!
Who's there?
Irving.
Irving who?
Irving a wonderful time,
wish you were here.

KNOCK-KNOCK!
Who's there?
Island.
Island who?
Island in your backyard in
my parachute.

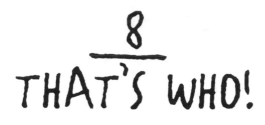

8
THAT'S WHO!

KNOCK-KNOCK!
Who's there?
Jacklyn.
Jacklyn who?
Jacklyn Hyde were two crazy doctors.

KNOCK-KNOCK!
Who's there?
Janet.
Janet who?
Janet has too many holes in it.

KNOCK-KNOCK!
Who's there?
Jaws.
Jaws who?
Jaws stopped by to see if you want to go for a swim.

KNOCK-KNOCK!
  Who's there?
Jewel.
  Jewel who?
Jewel know who when
you open the door.

KNOCK-KNOCK!
  Who's there?
July.
  July who?
July to me
about stealing
my piggy bank?

9
DOOR SLAMMERS!

KNOCK-KNOCK!
Who's there?
Kansas.
Kansas who?
Kansas the best way
to buy soup.

KNOCK-KNOCK!
Who's there?
Kermit.
Kermit who?
Kermit a crime, and the police'll lock you up.

KNOCK-KNOCK!
Who's there?
Knoxville.
Knoxville who?
Knoxville always get someone to
open the door.

KNOCK-KNOCK!
Who's there?
Lemon juice.
Lemon juice who?
Lemon juice you to my friend.

KNOCK-KNOCK!
Who's there?
Lena.
Lena who?
Lena little closer and I'll tell you a joke.

KNOCK-KNOCK!
Who's there?
Lauren.
Lauren who?
Lauren order.

KNOCK-KNOCK!

Who's there?

Lewis.

Lewis who?

Lewis all my money
to the school bully.

KNOCK-KNOCK!

Who's there?

Llama.

Llama who?

"Llama Yankee Doodle Dandy. . . ."

KNOCK-KNOCK!

Who's there?

Lucerne.

Lucerne who?

Lucerne some new words today?

KNOCK-KNOCK!

Who's there?

Lyndon.

Lyndon who?

Lyndon ear and I'll tell you a secret.

10
ORANGE YOU GLAD I DIDN'T SAY BANANA?

KNOCK-KNOCK!
  Who's there?
Mandy.
  Mandy who?
Mandy
lifeboats!
The ship is
sinking!

KNOCK-KNOCK!
Who's there?
Manatee.
Manatee who?
Manatee you made needs more lemon and sugar.

KNOCK-KNOCK!
Who's there?
Manicures.
Manicures who?
Manicures the sick is a doctor.

KNOCK-KNOCK!
Who's there?
Moo.
Moo who?
Well, make up your mind. Are you a cow or an owl?

KNOCK-KNOCK!
Who's there?
Myron.
Myron who?
Myron around the track made me tired.

KNOCK-KNOCK!
Who's there?
Nuisance.
Nuisance who?
I don't know. What's nuisance yesterday?

KNOCK-KNOCK!
Who's there?
Oil change.
Oil change who?
Oil change. Just give me a chance.

KNOCK-KNOCK!
Who's there?
Oliver.
Oliver who?
Oliver friends are on vacation.

KNOCK-KNOCK!
Who's there?
Omar.
Omar who?
"Omar darling, Clementine."

$$E = MC^2$$

KNOCK-KNOCK!
Who's there?
Omelet.
Omelet who?
Omelet smarter than I look.

KNOCK-KNOCK!
Who's there?
Onya.
Onya who?
Onya mark, get set, go!

KNOCK-KNOCK!
Who's there?
Ooze.
Ooze who?
Ooze in charge of this class?

KNOCK-KNOCK!
Who's there?
Oscar.
Oscar who?
Oscar for an "A" and the teacher might give it to you.

KNOCK-KNOCK!
Who's there?
Otter.
Otter who?
Otter see what I bought you.

KNOCK-KNOCK!
Who's there?
Ox.
Ox who?
Ox me for another piece of cake if you want one.

KNOCK-KNOCK!
Who's there?
Ozzie.
Ozzie who?
Ozzie you later.

11
SCHOOL OF HARD KNOCKS!

KNOCK-KNOCK!
Who's there?
Patsy.
Patsy who?
Patsy dog on the head. He likes it!

KNOCK-KNOCK!
Who's there?
Pasture.
Pasture who?
Pasture bedtime, isn't it?

KNOCK-KNOCK!
Who's there?
Pencil.
Pencil who?
Pencil vania's my favorite state.

KNOCK-KNOCK!
Who's there?
Philip.
Philip who?
Philip the candy bowl, I'm starving.

KNOCK-KNOCK!
Who's there?
Phyllis.
Phyllis who?
Phyllis in on the latest gossip.

KNOCK-KNOCK!
   Who's there?
Pudding.
   Pudding who?
Pudding your shoes on before
your pants is a bad idea.

KNOCK-KNOCK!
Who's there?
Rabbit.
   Rabbit who?
Rabbit up
carefully,
it's a birthday
present.

KNOCK-KNOCK!
Who's there?
Randy.
Randy who?
Randy four-minute mile in
less than three.

KNOCK-KNOCK!
Who's there?
Repeat.
Repeat who?
All right. Who. Who. Who.

KNOCK-KNOCK!
Who's there?
Rice.
Rice who?
Rice and shine, it's the first day of school.

KNOCK-KNOCK!
Who's there?
Ricotta.
Ricotta who?
Ricotta frog. Wanna see him jump?

KNOCK-KNOCK!
Who's there?
Roach.
Roach who?
Roach you a note in class,
but I never heard back.

KNOCK-KNOCK!
Who's there?
Roxanne.
Roxanne who?
Roxanne corals make the
aquarium look nice.

KNOCK-KNOCK!
Who's there?
Rufus.
Rufus who?
Rufus leaking and I'm getting wet!

KNOCK-KNOCK!
Who's there?
Russell.
Russell who?
Let's Russell up
something to eat.

KNOCK-KNOCK!

Who's there?

Russian.

Russian who?

Russian about will make you dizzy.

12
BAD RAP

KNOCK-KNOCK!
 Who's there?
Sahara.
 Sahara who?
Sahara you doing? I'm doing fine.

KNOCK-KNOCK!
Who's there?
Saddle.
Saddle who?
Saddle be the day!

KNOCK-KNOCK!
Who's there?
Sadie.
Sadie who?
Sadie Pledge of Allegiance.

KNOCK-KNOCK!
Who's there?
Samantha.
Samantha who?
Samantha baby have gone for a walk.

KNOCK-KNOCK!
Who's there?
Samoa.
Samoa who?
Samoa soda pop, please!

KNOCK-KNOCK!
Who's there?
Sarong.
Sarong who?
Sorry, I was sarong.

KNOCK-KNOCK!
Who's there?
Senior.
Senior who?
Senior report card and
it ain't all that good!

KNOCK-KNOCK!
   Who's there?
Seize her.
   Seize her who?
Seize her and Cleopatra.

>   **KNOCK-KNOCK!**
>   Who's there?
>   Shear.
>   Shear who?
>   Shear good to see you up and about.

KNOCK-KNOCK!
   Who's there?
Sheila.
   Sheila who?
"Sheila be coming around the mountain when she comes."

>   **KNOCK-KNOCK!**
>   Who's there?
>   Sherlock.
>   Sherlock who?
>   Sher, lock the doors. See if I care.

KNOCK-KNOCK!
Who's there?
Simon.
Simon who?
Simon the dotted line.

KNOCK-KNOCK!
Who's there?
Sincerely.
Sincerely who?
Sincerely this morning, I've been waiting for you to open this door.

KNOCK-KNOCK!
Who's there?
Stanton.
Stanton who?
Stanton here in the cold is no fun!

KNOCK-KNOCK!
Who's there?
Stop watch.
Stop watch who?
Stop watch you are doing and open the door.

KNOCK-KNOCK!
  Who's there?
Sultan.
  Sultan who?
Sultan pepper on steak tastes good.

KNOCK-KNOCK!
  Who's there?
Sweden.
  Sweden who?
Sweden sour is my
favorite Chinese soup.

KNOCK-KNOCK!
  Who's there?
Tamara.
  Tamara who?
Tamara is Tuesday.

KNOCK-KNOCK!
  Who's there?
Tennis.
  Tennis who?
Tennis five plus five.

KNOCK-KNOCK!
Who's there?
Thayer.
Thayer who?
Thayer sorry and I'll forgive you.

KNOCK-KNOCK!
Who's there?
Thelonius.
Thelonius who?
Thelonius kid in town.

KNOCK-KNOCK!
Who's there?
Thermos.
Thermos who?
Thermos be a better knock-knock joke than that last one.

KNOCK-KNOCK!
Who's there?
Tibet.
Tibet who?
"Early Tibet and early to rise. . . ."

KNOCK-KNOCK!
Who's there?
Thumpin'.
Thumpin' who?
Thumpin' slimy is
crawling up your back!

    KNOCK-KNOCK!
    Who's there?
    Tootle.
    Tootle who?
    Goodbye to you, too.

KNOCK-KNOCK!
Who's there?
Topic.
Topic who?
Topic a wildflower is against the law.

KNOCK-KNOCK!
Who's there?
Tummy.
Tummy who?
Tummy you'll
always be
number one.

KNOCK-KNOCK!
Who's there?
Tyrone.
Tyrone who?
Tyrone shoelaces.

13
BOO WHO?

KNOCK-KNOCK!
Who's there?
Uriah.
Uriah who?
Keep Uriah on the ball.

KNOCK-KNOCK!
Who's there?
Uruguay.
Uruguay who?
You go Uruguay and I'll go mine.

KNOCK-KNOCK!
Who's there?
Value.
Value who?
Value be my Valentine?

KNOCK-KNOCK!
Who's there?
Vaughan.
Vaughan who?
"Vaughan day, my prince will come."

KNOCK-KNOCK!
Who's there?
Veal chop.
Veal chop who?
Veal chop around and find
some bargains.

KNOCK-KNOCK!
Who's there?
Venice.
Venice who?
Venice your father
coming home?

KNOCK-KNOCK!

Who's there?

Victor.

Victor who?

Victor his pants bending over.

KNOCK-KNOCK!

Who's there?
Vivaldi.
Vivaldi who?
Vivaldi books, there's still
nothing to read.

KNOCK-KNOCK!
Who's there?
Waddle.
Waddle who?
Waddle you give me
for my birthday?

KNOCK-KNOCK!
Who's there?
Warner.
Warner who?
Warner you coming out to play?

KNOCK-KNOCK!
Who's there?
Water.
Water who?
Water our chances of
winning the lottery?

    KNOCK-KNOCK!
    Who's there?
    Wayne.
    Wayne who?
    Wayne we gonna eat? I'm starving!

KNOCK-KNOCK!
Who's there?
Weasel.
Weasel who?
"Weasel while you work!"

    KNOCK-KNOCK!
    Who's there?
    Weavish.
    Weavish who?
    "Weavish you a Merry Christmas...."

KNOCK-KNOCK!

Who's there?

Wendy Waiter

Wendy Waiter who?

Wendy Waiter gets here,
order me a soda.

KNOCK-KNOCK!

Who's there?

Wheelbarrow.

Wheelbarrow who?

Wheelbarrow some
money from Mom and Dad.

KNOCK-KNOCK!
Who's there?
Whom, Whom.
Whom, Whom who?
"Whom, Whom on the range, where
the deer and the antelope play...."

KNOCK-KNOCK!
Who's there?
Windows.
Windows who?
Windows the school bus come?
I'm freezing!

KNOCK-KNOCK!
Who's there?
Woodchuck.
Woodchuck who?
Woodchuck chuck wood
if a woodchuck could?

KNOCK-KNOCK!

Who's there?

Wiley.

Wiley who?

Wiley was sleeping,
the alarm clock went off.

KNOCK-KNOCK!
  Who's there?
Winnie.
  Winnie who?
Winnie gets home, tell him to take a bath.

KNOCK-KNOCK!
  Who's there?
Wooden.
  Wooden who?
Wooden it be nice if
I get an "A" in math?

KNOCK-KNOCK!
  Who's there?
Yachts.
  Yachts who?
Yachts up, doc?

KNOCK-KNOCK!
   Who's there?
Yolanda.
   Yolanda who?
Yolanda me money and I'll pay you back.

   KNOCK-KNOCK!
      Who's there?
   Zeus.
         Zeus who?
      Zeus house is this, anyway?

KNOCK-KNOCK!
   Who's there?
Zizi.
   Zizi who?
It's Zizi when you know how.

KNOCK-KNOCK!
Who's there?
Diesel.
Diesel who?
Diesel be the last knock-knock joke! I promise.

ABOUT THE AUTHORS

Matt Rissinger and Philip Yates are the founders of National Knock-Knock Day, celebrated each year on October 31. Their other books include *Cleverest Comebacks Ever, Totally Terrific Jokes, Greatest Jokes Ever, It's Not My Fault Because...*, *Best School Jokes Ever, World's Silliest Jokes,* and several more. Philip is the author of a picture book, *A Pirate's Night Before Christmas,* also published by Sterling.

Matt lives near Valley Forge, Pennsylvania, with his wife, Maggie, daughters Rebecca, Emily, and Abigail, their dog, Breaker, and cat, Cleo. Philip lives in Austin, Texas, with his wife, Maria, and their two cats, Sam and Johnnie.

Visit www.laugh-a-roni.com for more jokes and to learn even more about Matt and Philip and their work.